CHANGING LEAVES

8 POETIC PIANO SOLOS IN A-B-A FORM

BY CAROLYN C. SETLIFF

To the Student

A-B-A form (also called "ternary form") is a simple but important musical structure. You have probably already played several pieces in this form without realizing it! It is based on the concept of departure and return, contrast and repetition (sometimes the return to the A section is slightly different). You'll find that pieces in ABA form are often easier to memorize.

After playing the solos in this collection, start analyzing all your other pieces and decide which of them have ABA forms!

Contents

ISBN 978-1-5400-7253-5

EXCLUSIVELY DISTRIBUTED BY

WILLIS MUSIC

HAL•LEONARD®

Visit Hal Leonard Online at
www.halleonard.com

Contact us:
Hal Leonard
7777 West Bluemound Road
Milwaukee, WI 53213
Email: info@halleonard.com

In Europe, contact:
Hal Leonard Europe Limited
42 Wigmore Street
Marylebone, London, W1U 2RN
Email: info@halleonardeurope.com

In Australia, contact:
Hal Leonard Australia Pty. Ltd.
4 Lentara Court
Cheltenham, Victoria, 3192 Australia
Email: info@halleonard.com.au

Full of Grace

Stepping lightly, full of grace
Smooth as silk, at a perfect pace.

Carolyn C. Setliff

Swaying gently

3

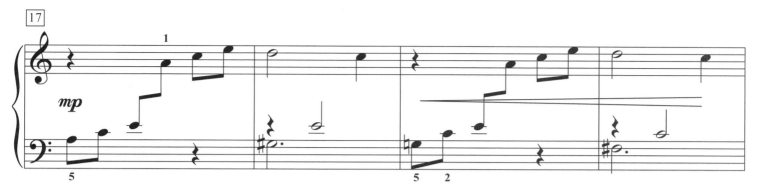

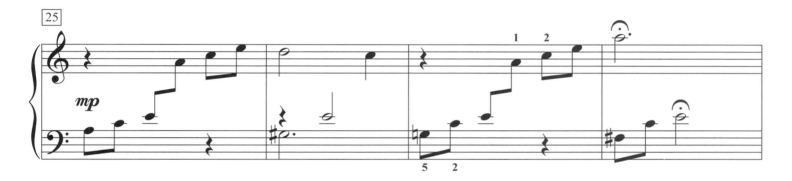

D.C. al Coda **CODA**

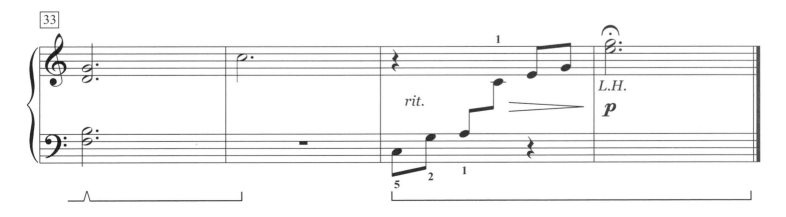

Changing Leaves

Take the back roads, not the highway
To see the little things:
The fields of corn, the changing leaves
And what adventure brings.

-Lori Jessen

Carolyn C. Setliff

Thoughtfully

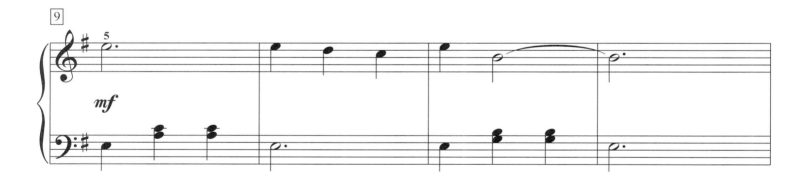

Fine

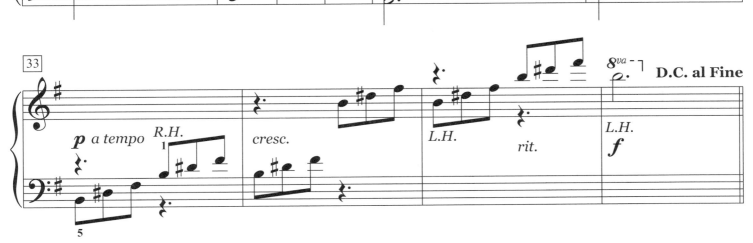

Seaside Reverie

Sitting on the shore
In a daydream...
The waves gently lap.

Carolyn C. Setliff

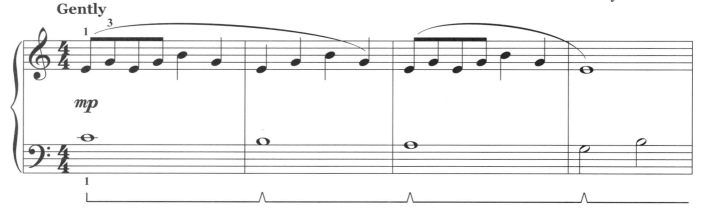

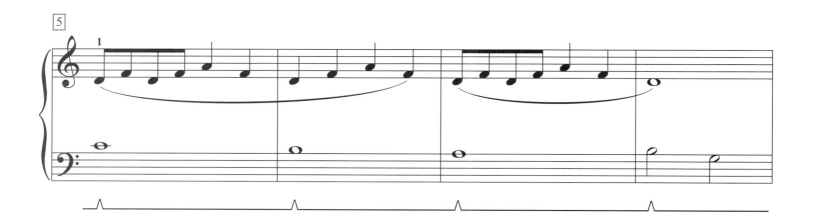

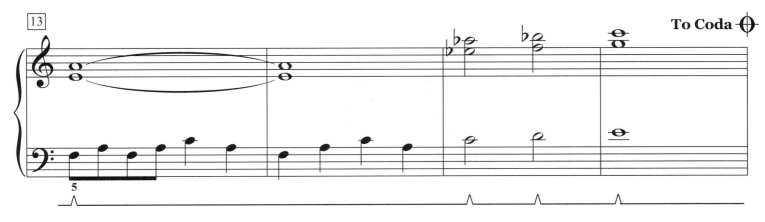

To Coda

D.C. al Coda

CODA

Summer Breeze

A summer breeze blows gently
Cooling, restoring.

Carolyn C. Setliff

Shamrock Glow

At rainbow's end
Green shamrocks grow
Planted in a pot of gold.

Carolyn C. Setliff

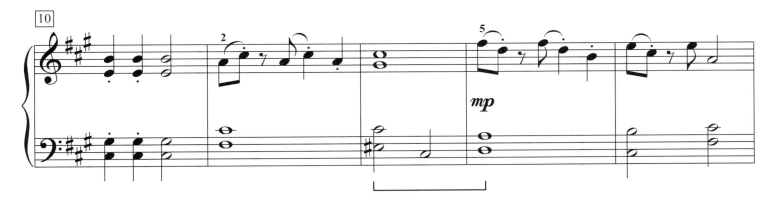

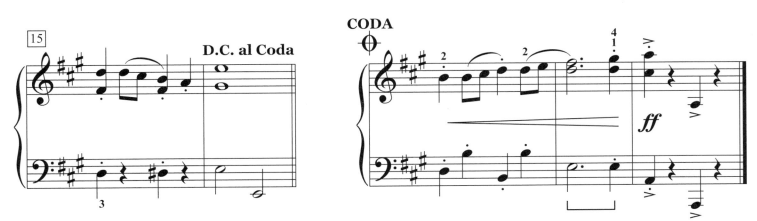

for Molly Priddle

Wind in My Hair

Fragrance of blooms
Wind in my hair
Sun on my back
My happy place.

Carolyn C. Setliff

Sparkling Sunbeams

Sunbeams glisten from on high
Shining forth from the blue sky
Into the trees they dance and dart:
Light without a sound.

Carolyn C. Setliff

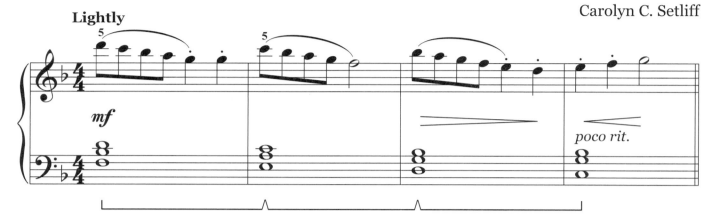

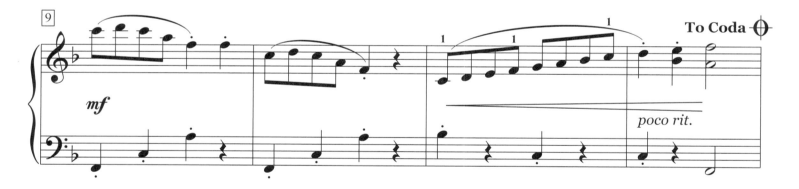

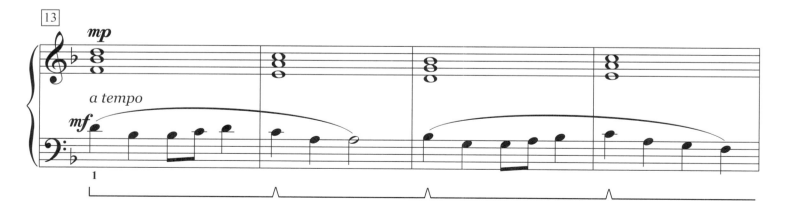

13

D.S. al Coda

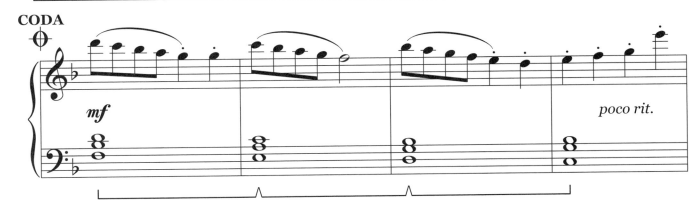

Gondola Ride

In Venice, Italy
A soft love song is heard
Down a narrow lagoon.

Carolyn C. Setliff

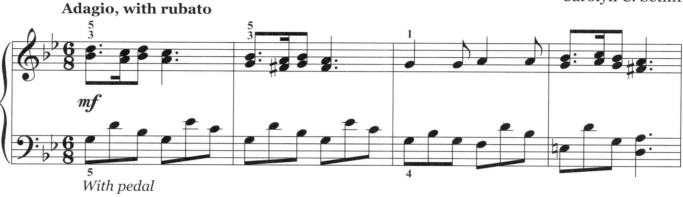

Carolyn C. Setliff is a composer and teacher from Little Rock, Arkansas and is an active member of local, state, and national music teacher associations. She and her twin sister both followed closely in the footsteps of their mother, who was a piano teacher and church organist. Today, her daughter Cathy continues the family tradition and also teaches piano!

In her spare time, Carolyn loves to read, spend time with her grandkids, and travel.